POPULAR SONGS

HAL LEONARD
STUDENT PIANO LIBRARY

Irving Berlin Piano Duos

Three Favorite Songs Arranged for Two Pianos, Four Hands

Arranged by Don Heitler and Jim Lyke

CONTENTS

2   Cheek to Cheek
from the RKO Radio Motion Picture TOP HAT

9   They Say It's Wonderful
from the Stage Production ANNIE GET YOUR GUN

16   You're Just in Love
from the Stage Production CALL ME MADAM

ISBN 978-1-4234-9974-9

Irving Berlin Music Company®
www.irvingberlin.com

EXCLUSIVELY DISTRIBUTED BY

HAL•LEONARD®
CORPORATION
7777 W. BLUEMOUND RD. P.O. BOX 13819 MILWAUKEE, WI 53213

© Copyright 2010 by the Estate of Irving Berlin
International Copyright Secured   All Rights Reserved

For all works contained herein:
Unauthorized copying, arranging, adapting, recording, Internet posting, public performance,
or other distribution of the printed music in this publication is an infringement of copyright.
Infringers are liable under the law.

Irving Berlin logo and Irving Berlin Music Company are registered trademarks of the Estate of Irving Berlin.

Visit Hal Leonard Online at
www.halleonard.com

Cheek to Cheek

from the RKO Radio Motion Picture TOP HAT

Words and Music by IRVING BERLIN
Arranged by Don Heitler and Jim Lyke

© Copyright 1935 by Irving Berlin
Copyright Renewed
This arrangement © Copyright 2011 by the Estate of Irving Berlin
International Copyright Secured   All Rights Reserved

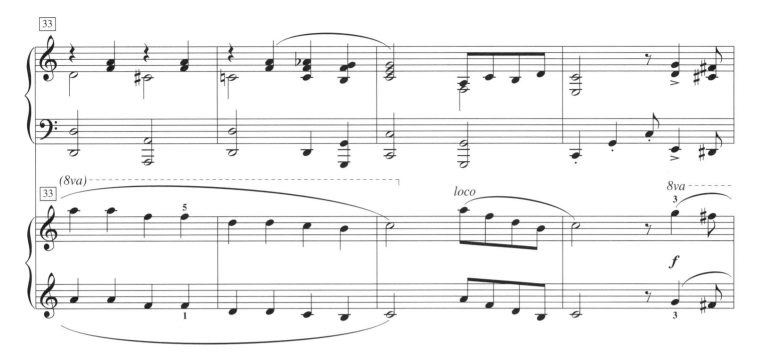

They Say It's Wonderful

from the Stage Production ANNIE GET YOUR GUN

Words and Music by IRVING BERLIN
Arranged by Don Heitler and Jim Lyke

© Copyright 1946 by Irving Berlin
Copyright Renewed
This arrangement © Copyright 2011 by the Estate of Irving Berlin
International Copyright Secured   All Rights Reserved

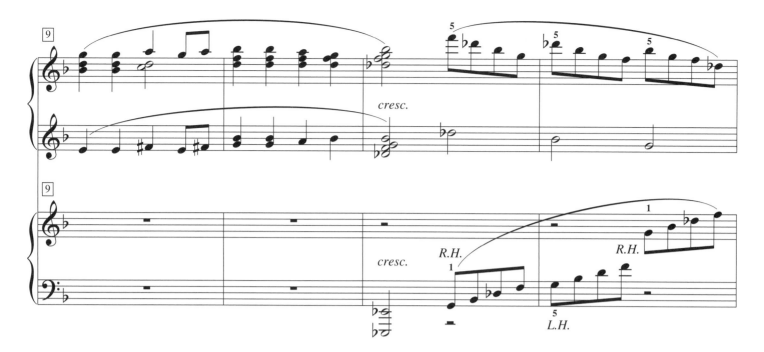

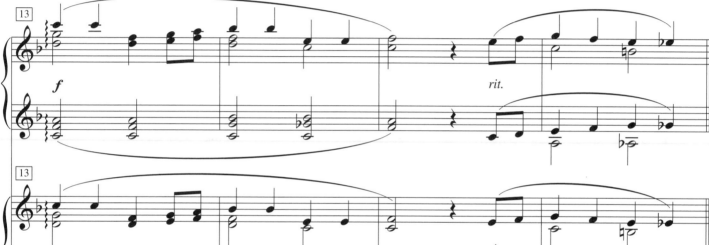

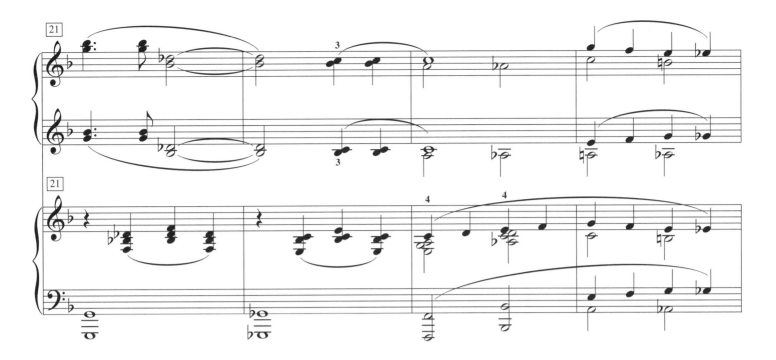

(I Wonder Why?)
You're Just in Love
from the Stage Production CALL ME MADAM

Words and Music by IRVING BERLIN
Arranged by Don Heitler and Jim Lyke

© Copyright 1950 by Irving Berlin
Copyright Renewed
This arrangement © Copyright 2011 by the Estate of Irving Berlin
International Copyright Secured   All Rights Reserved

POPULAR SONGS

HAL LEONARD STUDENT PIANO LIBRARY

TWO PIANOS, FOUR HANDS – LATE INTERMEDIATE LEVEL

Irving Berlin Piano Duos

Three Favorite Songs Arranged for Two Pianos, Four Hands

Arranged by Don Heitler and Jim Lyke

CONTENTS

2   Cheek to Cheek
from the RKO Radio Motion Picture TOP HAT

9   They Say It's Wonderful
from the Stage Production ANNIE GET YOUR GUN

16   You're Just in Love
from the Stage Production CALL ME MADAM

ISBN 978-1-4234-9974-9

Irving Berlin Music Company®
www.irvingberlin.com

EXCLUSIVELY DISTRIBUTED BY

HAL•LEONARD®
CORPORATION

7777 W. BLUEMOUND RD. P.O. BOX 13819 MILWAUKEE, WI 53213

© Copyright 2010 by the Estate of Irving Berlin
International Copyright Secured   All Rights Reserved

For all works contained herein:
Unauthorized copying, arranging, adapting, recording, Internet posting, public performance,
or other distribution of the printed music in this publication is an infringement of copyright.
Infringers are liable under the law.

Irving Berlin logo and Irving Berlin Music Company are registered trademarks of the Estate of Irving Berlin.

Visit Hal Leonard Online at
www.halleonard.com

Cheek to Cheek

from the RKO Radio Motion Picture TOP HAT

Words and Music by IRVING BERLIN
Arranged by Don Heitler and Jim Lyke

© Copyright 1935 by Irving Berlin
Copyright Renewed
This arrangement © Copyright 2011 by the Estate of Irving Berlin
International Copyright Secured   All Rights Reserved

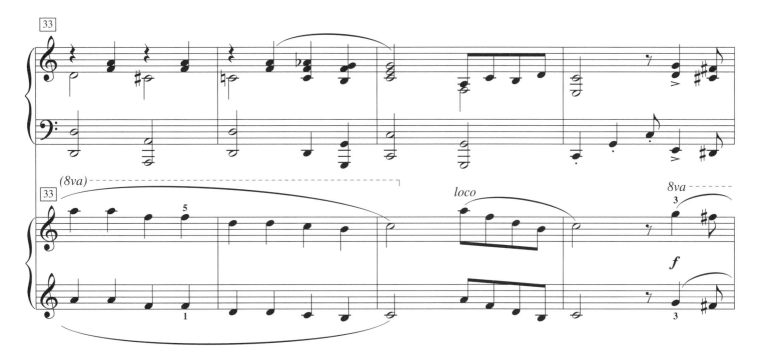

7

They Say It's Wonderful

from the Stage Production ANNIE GET YOUR GUN

Words and Music by IRVING BERLIN
Arranged by Don Heitler and Jim Lyke

© Copyright 1946 by Irving Berlin
Copyright Renewed
This arrangement © Copyright 2011 by the Estate of Irving Berlin
International Copyright Secured   All Rights Reserved

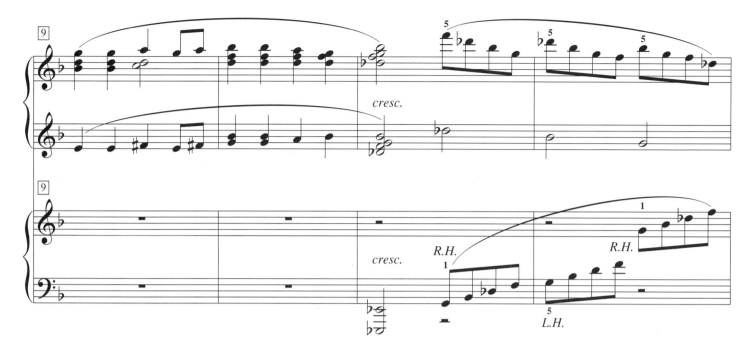

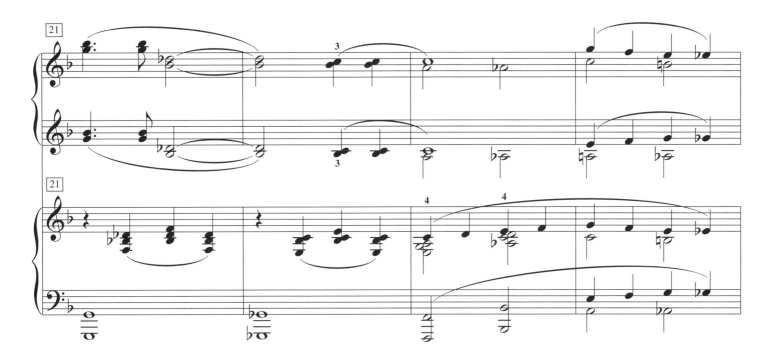

11

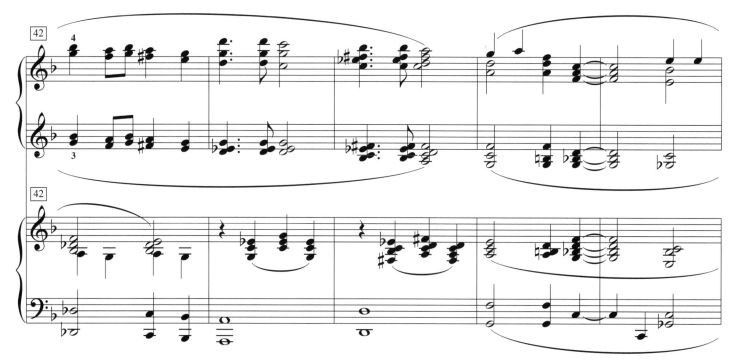

15

(I Wonder Why?)
You're Just in Love
from the Stage Production CALL ME MADAM

Words and Music by IRVING BERLIN
Arranged by Don Heitler and Jim Lyke

© Copyright 1950 by Irving Berlin
Copyright Renewed
This arrangement © Copyright 2011 by the Estate of Irving Berlin
International Copyright Secured   All Rights Reserved

(L.H. detached)

18

21

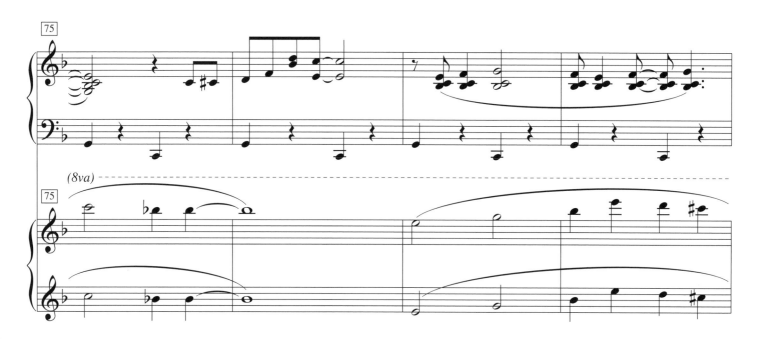

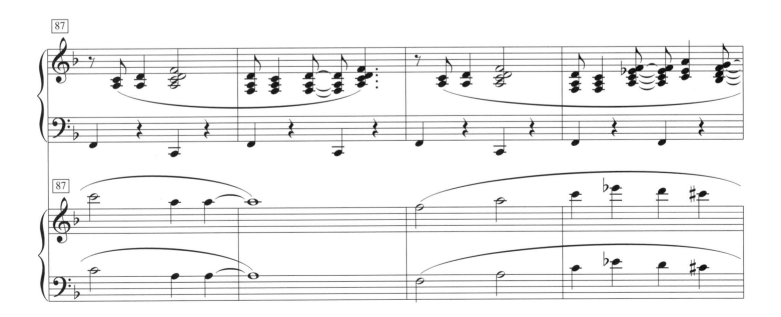

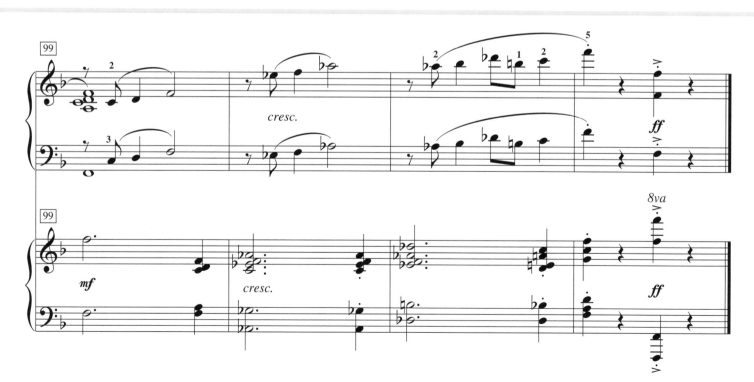

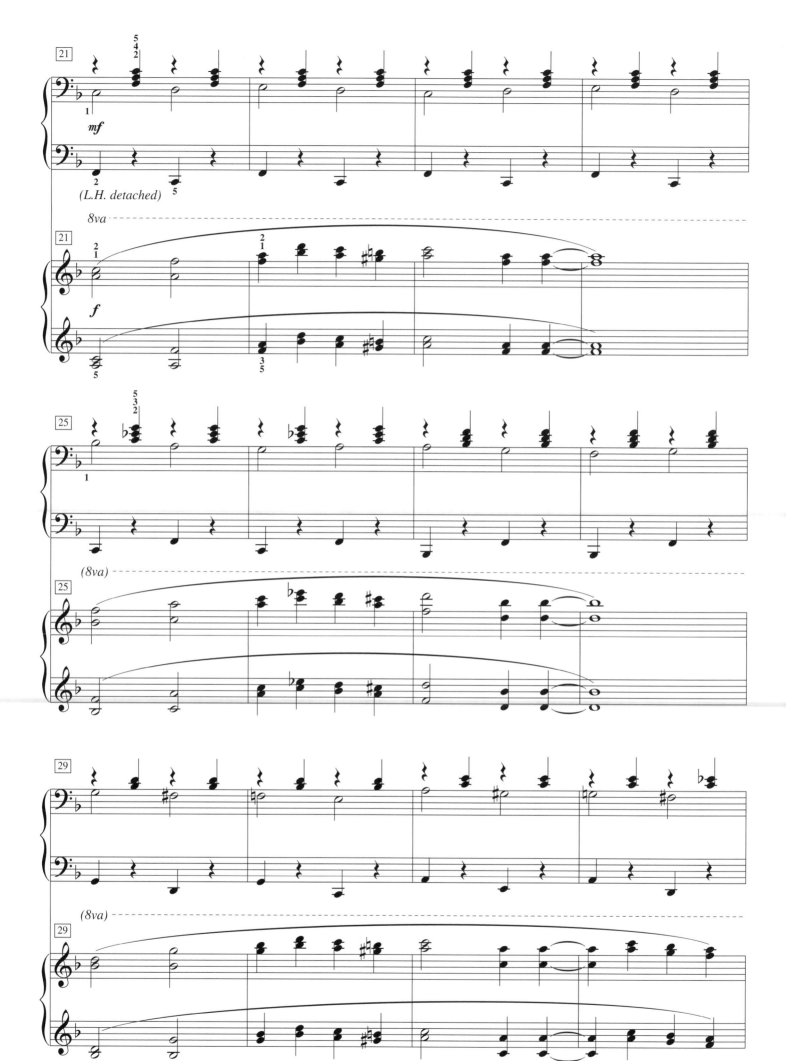

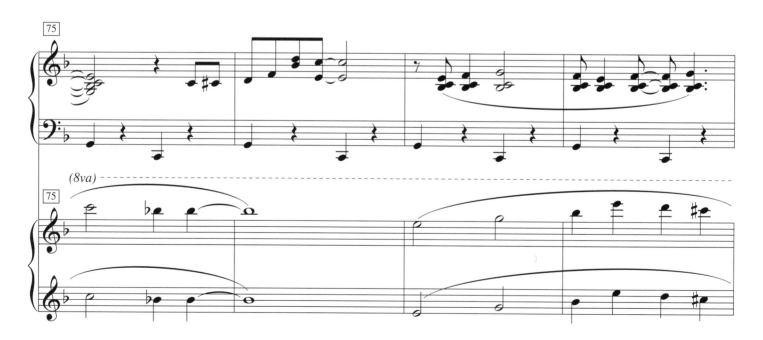

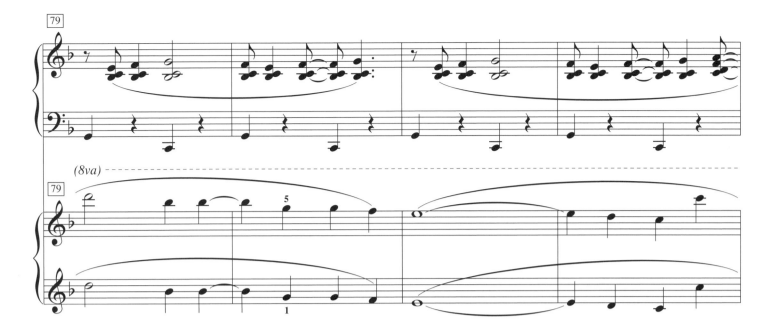